Philippines
the people

Greg Nickles

A Bobbie Kalman Book

The Lands, Peoples, and Cultures Series

Crabtree Publishing Company

www.crabtreebooks.com

The Lands, Peoples, and Cultures Series

Created by Bobbie Kalman

Coordinating editor
Ellen Rodger

Project editor
Carrie Gleason

Production coordinator
Rosie Gowsell

Project development, photo research, and design
First Folio Resource Group, Inc.
Erinn Banting
Tom Dart
Söğüt Y. Güleç
Alana Lai
Debbie Smith

Editing
Carolyn Black

Prepress and Printing
Worzalla Publishing Company

Consultants
Maria Genitrix P. Nañes, Philippine Consulate General (Toronto)

Photographs
Associated Press, AP: p. 15 (right); Melvin Calderon/ Liason/Hulton/Archive: p. 10 (right); Corbis/Magma Photo News Inc.: p. 8 (left); Corbis/Magma Photo News Inc./Paul Almasy: p. 13 (bottom); Corbis/Magma Photo News Inc./Bettmann: p. 9 (bottom), p. 10 (left); Corbis/ Magma Photo News Inc./Dean Conger: p. 14 (left); Corbis/ Magma Photo News Inc./Jay Directo, AFP: p. 14 (right); Corbis/Magma Photo News Inc./Michael Freeman: p. 19 (right); Corbis/Magma Photo News Inc./Romeo Gacad, AFP: p. 4 (top); Corbis/Magma Photo News Inc./Catherine Karnow: p. 11 (left); Corbis/Magma Photo News Inc./ Charles & Josette Lenars: p. 27 (bottom); Corbis/Magma Photo News Inc./Reuters NewMedia Inc.: p. 25 (bottom), p. 28 (right); Corbis/Magma Photo News Inc./Paul A. Souders: p. 12, p. 16 (left), p. 17 (left), p. 27 (top), p. 28 (left), p. 29 (top), p. 30 (both); Corbis/Magma Photo News Inc./Lito C. Uyan: p. 26 (right); Corbis/Magma Photo News Inc./Michael S. Yamashita: p. 22; Stuart Dee: cover; Mark Downey/ Lucid Images: p. 11 (right), p. 16 (right), p. 18, p. 19 (bottom left), p. 20 (bottom), p. 23 (bottom), p. 24 (bottom), p. 25 (top), p. 29 (bottom); Nancy Durrell-McKenna/Panos Pictures: p. 23 (top); Aaron Favila/ Associated Press, AP: p. 21 (left); Tom & Michele Grimm /International Stock: p. 5 (bottom); Jeremy Horner/Panos Pictures: p. 19 (top left); Hulton/Archive: p. 7 (right), p. 9 (top); Jay Ireland & Georgienne Bradley/ Bradleyireland.com: p. 20 (top); Henry Jayme: p. 24 (top); Stuart Norgrove/Life File: p. 13 (top), p. 17 (right); North Wind Pictures: p. 6, p. 7 (left), p. 8 (right); Corky Pasquil/ mybarong.com: p. 26 (left); Porterfield/ Chickering/Photo Researchers: p. 4 (bottom); Pat Roque/Associated Press, AP: p. 15 (left); Blair Seitz/ Photo Researchers: p. 3; Chris Stowers/Panos Pictures: title page, p. 5 (top), p. 21 (right); Flora Torrance/Life File: p. 31

Illustrations
Diane Eastman: icon
David Wysotski, Allure Illustrations: back cover

Cover: This Yakan woman lives in Zamboanga, on the island of Mindanao. The Yakan are well-known for the colorful handwoven textiles they create.

Title page: People carrying fresh fruits and vegetables cross a rickety bridge on their way home from a village market on the island of Luzon.

Icon: A house on stilts, one of the many types of homes in the Philippines, appears at the head of each section.

Back cover: Pangolins are mammals that are covered in hard scales. When threatened, they roll into a ball and use their scales to defend themselves.

Published by
Crabtree Publishing Company

PMB 16A,	612 Welland Avenue	73 Lime Walk
350 Fifth Avenue	St. Catharines	Headington
Suite 3308	Ontario, Canada	Oxford OX3 7AD
New York	L2M 5V6	United Kingdom
N.Y. 10118		

Cataloging in Publication Data
Nickles, Greg, 1969-
Philippines. The people / Greg Nickles.
p. cm. -- (The lands, peoples, and cultures series)
"A Bobbie Kalman book."
Includes index.
Summary: Examines the lives of the Filipine people: their families and traditions, life in the countryside and in cities, sports and pastimes, clothing, foods, and more.
ISBN 0-7787-9353-2 (RLB) -- ISBN 0-7787-9721-X (pbk.)
1. Philippines--Description and travel--Juvenile literature.
[1. Philippines--Social life and customs.] I. Title. II. Series.
DS663 .N53 2002
959.9--dc21
2001047110
LC

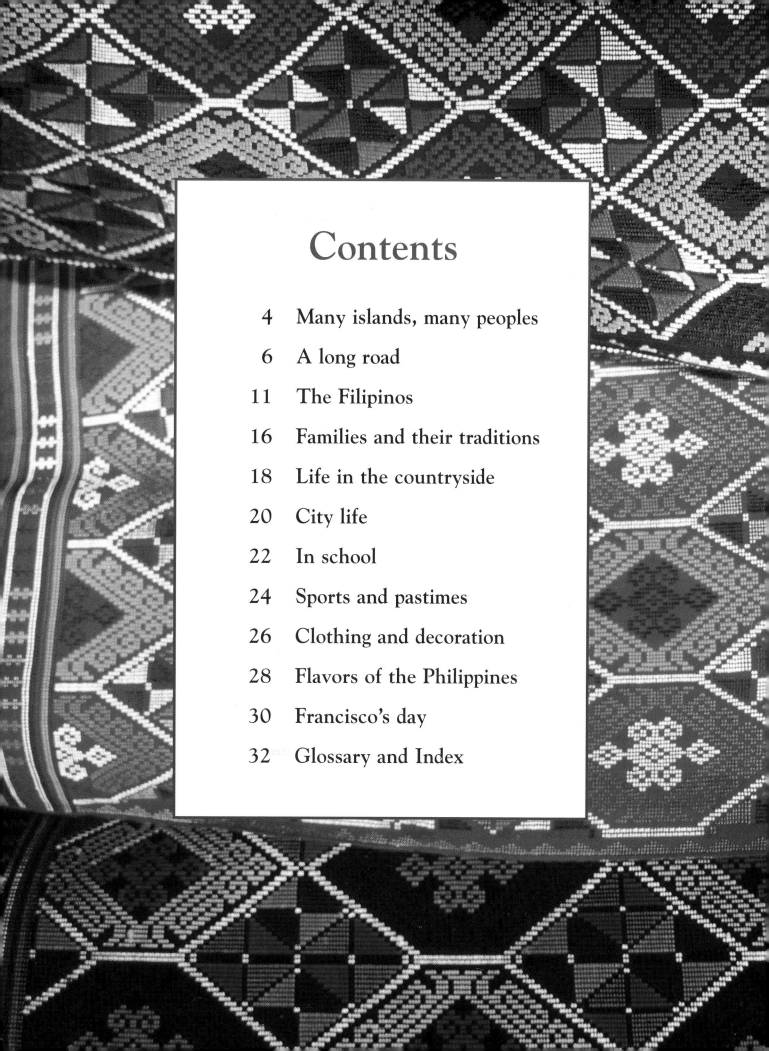

Contents

 # Many islands, many peoples

The people of the Philippines, called Filipinos, live in a country that is an **archipelago**, located off the coast of Southeast Asia. Mountains, plains, and dense rainforests cover the islands, and clear, blue oceans surround them.

Filipinos are a group of many peoples with different histories and cultures. They live in bustling cities, quiet towns, and isolated villages scattered across the country. Most Filipinos live peacefully together, but the differences between groups have occasionally led to fighting. Poverty and government **corruption** also cause problems. Whatever their background, Filipinos are united in wanting a peaceful country, a fair government, and better homes, schools, and jobs.

(top) Four girls wearing traditional costumes and headdresses made from hundreds of colorful beads perform a dance at the opening of a new park in Makati City, on the northern island of Luzon.

Sorting and bagging rice in the hot sun is tiring work. Rice is grown in paddies, or fields, in many parts of the Philippines.

These children, from the central island of Cebu, are eating bananas that were packed in crates to be shipped around the world. Bananas are one of the main crops grown in the Philippines.

This vendor displays butchered meat at the Puerto Princessa Market on the southwestern island of Palawan.

Over thousands of years, peoples from islands surrounding the Philippines settled the archipelago. Some historians believe that the first people of the Philippines were the Negrito, who crossed a land bridge from the nearby islands of Borneo and Sumatra more than 25,000 years ago. The Malay peoples from Indonesia and Malaysia started to migrate by boat to the Philippines a few thousand years ago. The Malay are the **ancestors** of most modern-day Filipinos.

As different groups of people came to the islands, they settled in small communities called *barangay*. Each *barangay* was ruled by a separate chief and developed its own language, traditions, and religious beliefs. Some *barangay* had close ties with other communities, others fought against one another.

From Asia and the islands

Chinese sailors began visiting the Philippines a thousand years ago to trade silk, glass, and other goods for the Filipinos' pearls, cotton, and tortoiseshells. They brought valuable knowledge to the Filipinos, including methods of writing and building. In the 1200s, Muslims came to the southern Philippines from nearby islands and introduced many Filipinos to their religion. Muslims are followers of Islam, the religion based on the teachings of God whom they call *Allah*, and his **prophet** Muhammad. These teachings are found in the holy book called the *Qur'an*, which is written in the Arabic language.

(top) This drawing from the 1400s shows a village at the bottom of Mount Mayon, on Luzon. The homes in the village are made from bamboo stalks and palm leaves.

Magellan's visit

In 1521, a European explorer named Ferdinand Magellan arrived in the Philippines from Spain. He was trying to sail around the world — something that no one had ever done before. Magellan and his crew visited a few Philippine islands before landing on the central island of Cebu. There, Magellan befriended the local people and agreed to help them attack their enemy, a leader named Lapu-Lapu on the nearby island of Mactan. Lapu-Lapu's soldiers won the battle and Magellan was killed. Some people in the Philippines consider Lapu-Lapu a national hero for defeating the Spanish.

Spanish invasion

Over the next 40 years, Spanish explorers continued to visit the archipelago. They named the whole area the "Philippines" after their prince, Philip. When Philip became king, he decided to make the islands a Spanish **colony**, from which Spanish ships could trade goods with China.

King Philip's soldiers took Cebu by force, and in 1565, they set up the first permanent Spanish settlement there. Afterward, they took control of most of the Philippines and its peoples.

Magellan and his crew help the people of Cebu battle Lapu-Lapu's soldiers in the Pacific Ocean, off the coast of Mactan, in this drawing from the 1500s.

A colony of Spain

The Spanish ruled the Philippines for more than 300 years. They built cities, often on the ruins of Filipino villages they had destroyed. Along with Spanish soldiers, merchants, and governors, **missionaries** from the Roman Catholic Church came to the Philippines to introduce the local people to Christianity. Roman Catholicism is a **denomination** of Christianity, a religion based on the teachings of Jesus Christ. Christians believe that Christ is the son of God.

The Spanish controlled government, business, and daily life in the Philippines. They forced Filipinos to follow European **customs** and traditions. A few Filipinos became wealthy landowners, merchants, or professionals, but most lived in poverty.

Treasure and pirates

Manila, on the northern island of Luzon, is the **capital** of the Philippines. During Spanish rule, it was an important **port** for traders who traveled between China and the Spanish colony of Mexico. China traded precious spices, silks, and other treasures for silver and gold from Mexico. The main ships that carried the riches between the two countries were known as the Manila galleon. Hauling treasure was dangerous. The Manila galleon and other Spanish ships became the targets of pirates. The pirates stole the ships' riches, and often sold crews into slavery in other lands. The Manila galleon trade continued until 1815.

Merchants and ships crowd Manila's port in this drawing from the 1800s.

Fighting for independence

By the late 1800s, Filipinos wanted to control their own government and end Spanish rule. José Rizal was a very popular doctor and writer who campaigned for better laws and living conditions for his people. As a result, the Spanish arrested, tortured, and finally killed him in 1896. Shocked at the brutal treatment of Rizal and others, Filipinos prepared to fight the Spanish.

The Spanish-American War

Filipino **rebels** waged war against their Spanish rulers. At the same time, the United States declared war on Spain. After destroying a group of Spanish ships at Manila, American Admiral George Dewey joined forces with the Filipino rebels. Together, Filipinos and Americans defeated the remaining Spanish forces in the Philippines.

On June 12, 1898, Filipinos declared their independence from Spain and celebrated the birth of their country. They chose rebel leader Emilio Aguinaldo as their first president. Months later, the United States surprised Filipinos by signing the Treaty of Paris with Spain which ended the Spanish-American War. According to the treaty, the United States had purchased the Philippines for $20 million. Enraged, Aguinaldo led his soldiers into battle against the American forces, but was captured. The Philippines remained a colony, now ruled by the United States instead of Spain.

Dr. José Rizal wrote several novels that criticized Spanish rule, including **Noli me tangere,** *or* **Touch Me Not.**

In this painting from the late 1800s, U.S. navy ships approach Manila Bay. During the Battle of Manila Bay, on May 1, 1898, the U.S. navy destroyed the Spanish fleet.

American rule and World War II

American leaders planned to grant their colony its independence, one day. In the meantime, the United States encouraged American businesses to open in the Philippines. Factories, schools, and hospitals were built. Filipinos appreciated the improvements in health care, education, and technology, but still wanted to rule their own country.

As a step toward independence, Filipinos finally elected their own president, Manuel L. Quezon, in 1935. In late 1941, however, **World War II** affected the Philippines. Japanese soldiers, at war throughout Asia and the Pacific, attacked and took over the islands. For three years, the United States battled Japan to regain control of the Philippines. Cities and villages were devastated and more than a million Filipinos died before American and Filipino soldiers recaptured the islands early in 1945.

Crowds of spectators watch as American officials take down the American flag and raise the Philippine flag at a ceremony on July 4, 1946. The ceremony commemorated the end of American rule and the beginning of Philippine independence.

Their own country

The United States granted the Philippines full independence on July 4, 1946. In the following years, Filipinos worked hard to rebuild their country, while terrible poverty and corrupt leaders added to their problems. Groups of **guerrillas**, such as the Hukbalahap, or Huks, battled with soldiers and the police. The Huks had helped fight the Japanese in World War II. After the war, they took up arms against wealthy land and business owners, who they believed caused the country's poverty.

Marcos takes control

In 1965, Filipinos elected a World War II hero named Ferdinand Marcos as president. Marcos promised to solve the country's problems, but he was very corrupt. Beginning in the 1970s, Marcos rigged the elections, so he always won. He also imprisoned or killed people who spoke out against him. Marcos and his wife Imelda lived in luxury, while other Filipinos suffered in poverty.

Marcos cast out

In 1983, Ferdinand Marcos was accused of having his popular opponent, Benigno Aquino, killed. Following Aquino's murder, his wife, Corazon, entered politics to lead the fight against Marcos. In 1986, Marcos tried to rig an election against Corazon Aquino. Millions of Filipinos were so outraged by their president's crimes that they held large demonstrations protesting his rule. The Philippine military sided with Aquino, and Ferdinand and Imelda Marcos fled the country, stealing billions of dollars from the Filipinos. Their theft remains one of the largest in history.

(above) Corazon Aquino was president of the Philippines from 1986 to 1992. During that time, she restored a democratic government to the Philippines, which meant that all Filipino citizens had the right to vote and participate in decisions made by the government.

The long road to recovery

After Marcos fled, Corazon Aquino became a hero and the new president. Filipinos hoped she could fix the country's problems, but these proved too big for just one leader. Powerful Marcos supporters attempted to kill Aquino and overthrow her government. Natural disasters, such as the massive eruption of the Pinatubo Volcano, followed in the 1990s. Aquino and later presidents have improved Filipinos' lives, but a great deal of work remains.

Ferdinand and Imelda Marcos pose for a photograph at the Malacañang Palace where they lived until 1986. Ferdinand Marcos died in 1989. His body now lies in a refrigerated mausoleum in the Ilocos region of Luzon. Imelda Marcos returned to the Philippines and was voted into parliament by people who had supported her husband.

More than 70 different ethnic groups live in the Philippines. Over the centuries, people from many of these ethnic groups **intermarried**. Today, the majority of Filipinos are Christians and live in the lowland areas. Tagalog and Cebuano peoples are the two largest groups of Filipinos, while smaller groups include the Ilocano, Hiligaynon, Bicolano, Waray-Waray, Pampango, and Pangasinan peoples. The Muslim and highland people have remained separate from the rest of the population and continue to lead traditional lifestyles.

Tagalog people

The Tagalog are the largest group of Filipinos, representing about one-quarter of the country's population. They live mostly on the plains of Luzon. Some Tagalog are farmers or fishers, while others live and work in cities such as Manila. For centuries, some of the most powerful politicians, businesspeople, and artists in the Philippines have been Tagalog. Their language, Tagalog, is the basis of Filipino, one of the Philippines' two official languages.

(below) These girls from Manila speak Tagalog. The Tagalog alphabet has 20 letters: 15 consonants and 5 vowels.

This Cebuano woman makes her way through a market while carrying fragrant spices in a basket on her head.

Cebuano people

The Cebuano, who make up almost another quarter of the population, are the second largest group of people in the Philippines. They live mostly in the cities and countryside of Cebu, although many have moved to other central islands and to the southern island of Mindanao. The Cebuano are active in politics, trade, music, and art. Like the Tagalog, most Cebuano are Christians, but they also believe in spirits, as their ancestors did. They perform rituals for these spirits and offer them gifts for good luck.

The Negrito

The Negrito inhabit the mountain highlands of Luzon. Many continue to live the nomadic lifestyle of their ancient ancestors. They build homes, hunt, fish, and grow crops in one place, then move to another place the next year. Many Negrito live in groups of three to ten families. The groups are led by the eldest man. Everyone works hard and gathers food daily to make sure the community survives.

Long ago, neighboring peoples, such as the Kalinga and Ifugao, killed the Negrito or sold them into slavery. To protect themselves, the Negrito moved to remote parts of the mountains. In 1991, the eruption of the Pinatubo Volcano killed many Negrito and destroyed parts of their lands. This disaster, combined with the cutting down of forests, forced some Negrito to give up their traditional lifestyle and move to Manila or to special communities that the government built in areas where the Negrito used to live.

Igorot peoples

The mountains of Luzon are home to the Igorot peoples. The name "Igorot" comes from the Tagalog word for "mountaineer." There are ten groups of Igorot. The largest are the Ifugao, Kalinga, Apayao, and Bontok. Most groups make their living tending large crops of rice.

The Ifugao

The Ifugao are famous around the world for the mountainside terraces where they have grown rice for 3,000 years. The terraces look like giant steps all around the mountains. The Igorot live in villages right on the terraces. Each village has about 30 people, with up to twelve dwellings. Daily life involves farming and practicing traditional ceremonies to honor more than 1,500 Ifugao gods.

A Negrito woman rests with her children and their cousins by the side of the road in Manila.

The Banaue rice terraces, behind this group of traditionally dressed Igorot men and women, cover more than 4,000 square miles (10,360 square kilometers).

The Kalinga, who live in the northern part of Luzon, are known for their rice farming, pottery, basketweaving, and metalwork.

The Kalinga

The Kalinga live in densely wooded areas, in villages with several small houses clustered together. They trade rice and other foods that they grow, as well as animals that they hunt in the surrounding forests. The Kalinga saying "Nothing happens that does not start from the hearth" expresses the Kalinga's belief that family is the most important thing in life.

Many years ago, the Kalinga were headhunters, like the Ifugao and several other Igorot peoples. They cut off the heads of their enemies and kept them as prizes. The United States outlawed this custom while the Philippines was its colony.

Manobo peoples

Manobo peoples live on Mindanao and in the Sulu Archipelago, a chain of islands that extends southwest from Mindanao. Unlike most Filipinos, the Manobo are Muslims. The main groups of Manobo include the Bajau, Tausug, Maguindanao, and Maranao.

The Bajau

The Bajau inhabit the Sulu Archipelago. They make their living by fishing and by trading handmade boats, pottery, and weaving. Many Bajau live in cities and towns, while others own small houses in seaside villages. A few live on their boats, in small "boat villages."

A Bajau fisher lifts a heavy net filled with fish out of the deep waters of the Celebes Sea.

Tausug boys beat the heat by jumping off a dock on Jolo Island, in the Sulu Archipelago.

The Tausug

The Tausug, whose name means "people of the sea **current**," live in small villages and towns throughout the Sulu Archipelago. They fish, grow crops, or trade goods such as coconut and abaca, or hemp, with nearby China. Abaca is used to make sturdy rope and fabrics.

Traditionally, the Tausug were known as strong warriors because they fended off Spanish attackers for over 300 years. Today, some Tausug belong to a group called the Moro National Liberation Front, or MNLF. The MNLF wants to separate from the Philippines and create its own country. Fierce battles occur between MNLF independence fighters and government troops.

Musicians play traditional Chinese instruments and dancers perform a dragon dance at a Chinese New Year's celebration in Manila.

People of Chinese ancestry

About one in every ten Filipinos has Chinese ancestors. These ancestors were traders who visited or settled in the Philippines hundreds of years ago. More recent Chinese immigrants also live in the country. While most Filipinos of Chinese ancestry do not have close ties with China, Chinese culture influences Filipino food, clothing, and **architecture**.

Filipinos abroad

More than 400 years ago, Spaniards forced Filipinos to work on Spanish ships sailing to Mexico and other Spanish colonies. Filipinos escaped from these ships and settled in the countries where the ships landed. More recently, Filipinos have moved to the United States, Japan, Canada, and the Middle East either to go to school or to find jobs.

Fact or fiction?

In 1971, the government of Ferdinand Marcos announced it had found a group of people called the Tasaday living in a rainforest cave on Mindanao. The government claimed that the Tasaday were an ancient people, and that the 26 remaining Tasaday knew nothing of the outside world. They wore leaves as clothes and survived by eating wild foods. This discovery was reported around the world, and brought the Philippines a great deal of attention.

In 1986, shocked reporters found the cave empty and the Tasaday living in a nearby village, dressed in modern clothes. They accused the government of making up the story about the long-lost Tasaday, as well as forcing poor, local farmers to pretend to be the Tasaday for newspaper and television reporters. The truth about the Tasaday is still debated today, although most people now believe the story was false.

This photograph from 1971 shows people who were believed to be Tasaday in the rainforests of Mindanao.

Families and their traditions

Filipino families enjoy special events together, such as this festival in Cebu.

Filipinos think of their families as a source of protection and strength. Family members look out for one another, especially when difficult times affect their country. Everyone works together to keep the family clothed, fed, and housed. In some households, older children work to pay for the education of their younger brothers and sisters. When not working, families have fun and enjoy many celebrations.

Dating and engagement

Filipino families are protective of children who are old enough to marry. Traditionally, parents had to approve of their daughter's date, and an older family member accompanied the couple wherever they went. If a couple wished to marry, the man's parents performed a custom called *pamanhikan*: they visited the woman's parents to formally request the marriage.

Before agreeing to the marriage, each family made sure that the other was known to be loyal and respectful. Today, these traditions are followed less often, especially in the cities.

Wedding traditions

Most Christian weddings in the Philippines take place in churches. One common tradition is for the groom to give the bride an *arras*, or collection of coins, as a sign that he will provide for her and their children. Sometimes, the coins are strung together on gold-plated wires for safekeeping because Filipinos consider it bad luck if the groom drops or loses them. Some grooms prefer to keep the coins loose, as a sign to their bride that they will be responsible husbands.

Among Muslim Filipinos, marriages are often arranged by the parents of the bride and groom. Only the groom attends the wedding ceremony, not the bride, but both join their friends and relatives for a party afterward. According to Tausug tradition, the groom and bride must sit motionless throughout the whole party!

*During a traditional Filipino Christian wedding ceremony, a white silk cord called a **yugal** is draped over the bride and groom's shoulders to form a figure eight. The **yugal** symbolizes a strong, everlasting bond between the couple.*

A funeral procession made up of neighbors, friends, and family follows a car through a mountain road near the town of Santa Fe, on Luzon.

Respect, honor, and *utang na loob*

Filipino parents teach their children important lessons about how to behave toward others. Children learn to treat their elders with great respect. They are taught the importance of doing favors for family members and close friends without being asked. In return, the receivers are bound by *utang na loob*, or "a debt of the inner self," and they try to generously repay the favor. Children also learn that when they are in a group, it is proper to respect *pakikisama*, or a sense of friendliness and togetherness. It is rude to disagree openly with the group or to refuse to go along with what the group wants.

Laid to rest

After a Christian Filipino dies, his or her body lies in the family home for several days. Relatives come from far away to pay their respects. Then, the family carries the body to church, accompanied by a brass band playing sad music. After the ceremony and burial, family and friends gather for nine nights to pray for the person who died.

Muslims believe people should be buried soon after death. If a Muslim Filipino dies, the family washes the body and wraps a white cloth around it. An *imam*, or prayer leader, helps with the burial.

Back from the dead

According to tradition, the Mangyan people, who live on the island of Mindoro, sometimes hold a *panludan* celebration to honor a dead family member. A year after a person dies, family members dig up the body and bind it in blankets. During the *panludan*, they sing, talk to, and pretend to feed the dead person. Later, they clean the person's bones and lay them to rest in a cave where the bones of other relatives lie.

A Mangyan woman wraps the bones of her ancestor in a brightly colored blanket.

Life in the countryside

Almost half of Filipinos live in the countryside, on plains, in mountain forests, or by the sea. Most live in small villages or towns. *Poblaciones* are small towns that the Spanish established long ago. From the *poblaciones*, people built roads that look like spokes extending from the middle of a wheel. Eventually, larger towns called *barrios* sprang up along these roads.

Many kinds of homes

Rural Filipinos live in several kinds of homes. A *bahay kubo*, or "cube house," is a traditional rural home. Its walls and floors are made of **bamboo** and palm leaves. Woven palm leaves and grass form the roof. A *bahay kubo* stands above the ground on tall stilts. People need to climb a ladder to get inside! The stilts protect the home from dampness, flooding, and wild animals. **Livestock** is often kept underneath the home.

Other people in the countryside live in wooden homes with iron roofs. Houses made of brick, cement, or stone are common in towns. The homes of the few wealthy Filipinos who live in the countryside are large and fancy. They tend to be old mansions or more modern single-family houses.

On the inside

Most rural homes, especially in remote areas, have one main room with a few pieces of furniture and mats on the floor where the family sleeps. The kitchen, with a wood-burning stove, is in a second room. Many houses in larger towns have indoor plumbing and electricity, but these conveniences are rare in small villages. Instead, people gather water from a community well and burn **kerosene** lamps for light in the evening.

(top) A long walkway made from bamboo bound together with rope leads to the front of this **bahay kubo. *The walls of the house are also made from bamboo, and the roof is made from tightly woven* nipa, *or palm leaves.***

A young girl washes her hands at a community well near Digos, a village on Mindanao. Families also draw water from the well and carry it back to the village in large jugs to use for cooking and washing.

Homes on the water

Families in the south live along the sea, in homes raised on stilts over the water. There is usually one large room, with a kitchen in a separate building. To travel to and from their home, families use a boat, which they dock at a platform by their house.

Some Bajau families live on their boats. A light bamboo frame, with a roof made of palm leaves, covers the living and sleeping space. This area is about ten feet (three meters) long and four feet (one meters) wide. The family cooks its meal and stores drinking water in a separate area at the back of the boat.

At work

Rural Filipinos are mostly farmers, fishers, or craftspeople. Many people make their living doing a combination of jobs. Some use modern equipment, but it is expensive, so people often do their work by hand. Farmers use horses, oxen, and a kind of water buffalo called a carabao to help them with their work. In addition to the fish they catch or the crops they grow for sale, families grow their own food. They also raise chickens for eggs and pigs for meat.

(above) A carabao pulls a plow through a farmer's field. Once the field is plowed, the farmer will plant new crops.

(left) Homes on stilts are built high enough above the water to prevent floods during high tide or during a storm.

19

Philippine cities look very different from one another, depending on what part of the country they are in. Old Spanish churches, forts, and palaces rise in cities in the north. Minarets, or the prayer towers of Muslim **mosques**, dot cities in the south. Most buildings in cities are newer. These buildings replaced older buildings that were destroyed during World War II.

In the *plaza*

Life in cities revolves around *plazas*, which are large, open squares with trees, benches, statues, and fountains. *Plazas* are usually in the centers of cities or neighborhoods. Here, Filipinos meet friends, grab a snack, read, or take a nap. Sometimes, older buildings that survived the war, such as the main church or city hall, stand around the *plaza*. Several times a year, *plazas* and the surrounding streets come alive, as Filipinos celebrate *fiestas*, or festivals.

Puerto Princessa City, on Palawan, is one of the fastest-growing cities in the Philippines.

*The **plaza** is often a lively place where people gather to hear concerts.*

It is much faster to take a train than to drive during rush hour in Metropolitan Manila.

At home

Most people in cities live in small, comfortable houses or apartments with two or three rooms. Wealthy Filipinos have larger, more luxurious homes. The Filipino population is growing faster than affordable homes are built, so almost a third of people in cities cannot find or afford proper houses. Instead, they live in homes made of scraps of wood, cardboard, flattened tin cans, and whatever else they can find. Large neighborhoods of these types of homes are called shantytowns.

Working days

People in cities work at construction sites or at factories, where they manufacture textiles, clothing, electronics, and other goods for **export**. Other people pack and can seafood, vegetables, and fruit. Many professionals, such as teachers, lawyers, and scientists, work in the cities. Unfortunately, jobs are hard to find, even for people with a lot of training.

In the markets

Philippine cities have malls and supermarkets similar to those in North America, but many city dwellers go instead to the closest outdoor market to buy fabrics, flowers, fresh food, and just about anything else. People buy rice once a week, but shop for fresh vegetables, fruit, and seafood every day. For meat, they go to the "wet" market. There, the stalls and ground are wet with the water that **vendors** use to wash away blood from freshly killed livestock.

The *kasambahay*

In the city, a *kasambahay*, or household, is often larger than a *kasambahay* in the countryside. Housing in the city is very expensive, so children, parents, grandparents, aunts, uncles, and cousins often live together. If relatives from the countryside come to the city to study or work, they become part of the *kasambahay*, too.

Markets in many cities in the Philippines are very busy in the early morning and late afternoon, with people shopping on their way to and from work. During one of the slower times of the day, a merchant arranges her flowers at the market in Butuan City, on Mindanao.

In school

From June until March, Filipino children spend their days at school. Schools in cities are usually clusters of buildings with covered walkways connecting them. The classrooms surround courtyards, where children play at recess time. During the day, teachers leave windows and doors open to let cool breezes flow through the hot, crowded rooms. City schools can have up to 40 students in one class!

Schools in the countryside are smaller. Some of them have just one classroom, with a single teacher for students of all ages. The number of students varies depending on the time of year. There are fewer students during the harvest because children help their families gather crops.

(top) These boys attend a military school in Manila. They study the same subjects as children in public schools, including computer science, but have military training and will serve in the army when they graduate.

In class
Classes begin around eight in the morning, after students salute the flag, recite the Philippine Pledge of Allegiance, and sing the national anthem. They learn history, math, science, English, and Filipino in the morning, when it is cooler. They also take special lessons on the traditional cultures of the Filipino peoples. In the afternoon, children take courses in music, sports, **trades**, and practical subjects, such as cooking, sewing, or growing a vegetable garden. School ends around three in the afternoon, but some students stay later to play sports or participate in clubs.

Games new and old
Children play all sorts of games during breaks between classes and after school. They play basketball, volleyball, and video games, as well as traditional games that Filipino children have played for many years. *Piko* is a kind of hopscotch, *tanguan* is hide-and-seek, and *patintero* is tag. *Sipa* is a favorite game. Players form a circle and kick the *sipa*, a small mesh ball, back and forth. They try to keep it in the air as long as they can.

Tumbang preso

You can play a traditional Filipino game called *tumbang preso* with a few friends. To begin, set an empty can or plastic container on a safe patch of sand or dirt. Then, choose a *preso*, or prisoner, to guard the can while the other players stand about sixteen feet (five meters) away.

One by one, each player throws his or her shoe at the can, trying to knock it over. The *preso* tries to block the shoes. If a player knocks the can over, everyone rushes to pick up their shoes while avoiding the *preso*. If the *preso* tags someone, that person becomes the new *preso* and the game begins again.

Chemistry students watch an experiment at the Mindanao State University. There are over 60 universities and 1,000 colleges in the Philippines.

Challenges for education

The Philippines has a high literacy rate, which means that most people can read and write. Unfortunately, some children must drop out of school and work to help support their families. Other children attend schools that do not have enough desks, textbooks, or supplies.

Children play a popular game at a school in Manila. One child stands in the center of a circle while the other children sing and dance around him or her. When the song stops, the child in the center points to one of the children and they switch places.

Sports and pastimes

With so many sports and games to choose from, Filipinos can have a difficult time deciding what to watch and play. Like people around the world, they are big fans of tennis, boxing, swimming, and mountain climbing. Basketball is especially popular among both children and adults.

Ancient art

Arnis de mano is a Philippine **martial art**. It developed from another Philippine martial art called *kali*, which is about 2,000 years old. *Arnis de mano* is similar to sword fighting, but the fighters use different weapons. One weapon is the *balisong*, which is a knife that has a handle made from an animal's horn. Another weapon is the *tungkod*, a wooden stick that is about three feet (one meter) long. Competitors, wearing special protective equipment, sometimes fight with a weapon in each hand.

Two boys practice **arnis de mano** *moves using* **tungkods**, *while being supervised by their master.*

Teenagers play a game of basketball in a village on Palawan. Do you think this player will get the ball in the net?

Fighting roosters

Cockfighting, or *sabong*, is a popular spectator sport in the Philippines. Hundreds of people watch and place bets on two roosters fighting, usually to the death. The roosters peck one another with their beaks and slash each other with their claws. As the roosters furiously attack one another, audience members yell and cheer. Birds that do not survive their matches are often cooked in a dish called *talunan*, or the "loser's meal." Some people think that cockfighting is an act of cruelty to animals.

The yo-yo

Filipino children play with many toys, including spinning tops, kites, slingshots, dolls, and yo-yos. No one knows when the yo-yo, which means "come back" in Filipino, first appeared in the Philippines, but records from the 1500s suggest that hunters used a kind of yo-yo to catch animals for food. The hunters hid in trees and tangled the yo-yo's string around the legs of passing animals. In the 1920s, a Filipino named Pedro Flores introduced the yo-yo to the United States. Shortly afterward, a yo-yo company sprang up in California, and the toy became popular around the world.

To make the slashes more deadly during a cockfighting match, owners attach razors to their roosters' claws.

Maricris Fernandez, a professional tennis player from the Philippines, plays a match at the Southeast Asian Games in 1999.

Although most Filipinos wear the same kind of clothing that people wear in Europe or North America, they often dress in traditional costumes for *fiestas*. Some people in the countryside wear traditional clothing every day. These clothes are made from light fabrics, to keep Filipinos cool in the country's heat and humidity. Straw hats also protect people from the hot sun.

The *barong tagalog*

One of the main pieces of traditional clothing for men is the *barong tagalog*, or *barong* for short. The *barong* is a long, loose-fitting shirt. Men often wear a casual *barong tagalog* with short sleeves at work or at home. They save the long-sleeved *barong* with cuffs for formal events such as weddings.

Filipinos who live in cities dress in clothing that is similar to North American and European styles.

Decorating the *barong*

Many *barong* are decorated with handpainted patterns or embroidery. Embroidery is an old and respected art in the Philippines, which involves stitching fine, often brightly colored thread into patterns on cloth. Not everyone can afford the extremely expensive *barong tagalog* that is made from a fine silk cloth called *jusi* or a fabric called *piña*.

Piña from pineapple

Piña is a beautiful, **sheer**, brownish fabric that Filipinos weave by hand from the leaf fibers of wild pineapple plants. They select only the best leaves to make *piña*. After gently scraping the surface of the leaves to remove the fine fibers, they carefully tie the fibers together to form a single, continuous thread. They spin this thread around a spool, and then weave it into cloth on a loom.

Many people consider the **barong tagalog** *the national attire of the Philippines.*

Girls at a fiesta in Mandaue City, on Cebu, wear brightly colored ternos and headdresses. The headdresses are made from palm leaves and feathers that are woven together to look like flowers.

Kimona and terno

Some Filipino women wear a traditional blouse called a *kimona* that is decorated with fancy embroidery, like the *barong tagalog*. Women put their *kimona* over a long skirt and add a fragrant white sampaguita flower to their hair. Another traditional outfit for women is the *terno*, a long dress with puffy sleeves.

Bright colors

Muslim Filipinos wear traditional costumes decorated with bright colors. Important Maranao men, for example, have long, embroidered coats of yellow, maroon, or red. Tausug men and women wear a colorful tube skirt called a *patadyung*. Some Muslim women wear another kind of skirt called a *malong*. The *malong* is a wraparound skirt that comes in colors such as green, pink, or purple.

The tattoos on this Igorot woman, which are made of lines and designs, form a pattern that represents spiritual protection.

Body art

Until the middle of the 1900s, tattoos were popular among the Kalinga and other Filipino peoples in the countryside. Tattoo artists painted designs or pictures of people and animals under a person's skin. They used dyes made from plants as well as needle-like tools, including sharpened bird bones, seashells, or thorns. Even though receiving a tattoo was painful, it was considered an honor. Tattoos marked important events in a person's life, such as the passage into adulthood. Some Filipinos still receive traditional tattoo designs today.

Flavors of the Philippines

Filipinos usually eat dishes made from rice, corn, sweet potatoes, or other vegetables. A salty fish or shrimp sauce, called *patis*, seasons many foods. *Pan de sal*, a type of bun, is also a staple at mealtime, as are tropical fruits such as papaya, coconut, mango, and banana.

During large *fiestas*, Filipinos enjoy rich foods. A holiday favorite is *lechon*, a whole **suckling** pig that people roast over a fire. Another festive treat is fish, steamed and flavored with mayonnaise, relish, corn, parsley, and shredded carrots.

Bubbling broth

Filipinos cook a variety of soups, to which they add vegetables, rice, special noodles called *pancit*, or sometimes a little meat. They also prepare broths which are used to season other dishes. For example, the popular dish *sinigang* is a mixture of vegetables and meat or seafood. It cooks in a broth flavored with tamarind, a tropical fruit. The tamarind gives the other ingredients a delicious flavor that is both sour and sweet. Vinegar and garlic are also favorite seasonings for broths.

Lechon, *or roasted pigs, will be served during* **Ati-Atihan,** *a* **fiesta** *celebrated on the island of Panay.*

Adobo

Many people consider sweet, tangy *adobo* to be the Philippines' national dish. It is a stew made with a whole chicken or with pork. Garlic, vinegar, pepper, onions, and soy sauce add a strong flavor. *Adobo* simmers in a pot filled with oil, and is then served with rice or sweet potatoes.

Food on the street

For lunch or an afternoon snack, called *merienda*, people buy cobs of corn, peanuts, or mangoes from vendors with carts. Other vendors, who have permanent stalls or who work from their home, sell *pancit*, rice cakes, carabao cheese, and *lumpia*, which are like eggrolls. Another favorite treat is *balut*. *Balut* is a cooked duck egg with an unhatched duckling inside. People believe that eating *balut* gives them energy.

Pancit, *vegetables,* **adobo,** *and rice make a delicious meal.*

Vendors sell ice cream and other snacks to passengers on a bus and to passersby.

*This **halo halo** is made with vanilla ice cream, flavored shaved ice, bananas, sweet corn, coconut, and a maraschino cherry on top.*

Making *halo halo*

Halo halo, which means "all mixed up," is a popular dessert made with a mix of ingredients, including ice cream, milk, ice, fruit, corn, rice, and sweet red beans. The recipe below shows you just one way to make *halo halo*. Ask an adult to help. If you do not want corn, rice, or beans in your dessert, leave them out — just add more fruit cocktail.

For two servings, you will need:
• 2 sundae glasses and 2 spoons
• ice cream scoop
• 1 can fruit cocktail, chilled
• 1 small can sweet corn, drained and chilled
• 1 small can mung or sweet red kidney beans, drained and chilled
• 1/2 cup (125 ml) cooked white rice, chilled
• 1 can evaporated milk
• leche flan (baked custard) or vanilla ice cream
• shaved ice (If you do not have an ice shaver, place ice in a plastic bag and bang the bag on the floor.)
• shredded coconut
• pili nuts (optional)

What to do:
1. Put a scoop of fruit cocktail in the bottom of each glass. Pour some of the cocktail syrup over the fruit.

2. Layer a half-scoop each of corn, beans, and rice on top of the fruit cocktail.

3. Fill glasses almost to the top with shaved or crushed ice.

4. Pour in milk until it almost covers the ice.

5. Top each glass with a half-scoop of leche flan or a scoop of ice cream.

6. Sprinkle coconut and pili nuts on top.

Francisco kept yawning as he sang the national anthem with his classmates. He had not slept well since his cousins from the countryside arrived to stay with his family. "Why do they get my bed, and I get a floor mat?" he muttered, as he sat down.

A gentle poke in his back made him jump. Francisco turned and frowned at Dona, the girl at the desk behind him. "Talking to yourself again?" Dona whispered with a smirk.

Francisco groaned and rubbed his eyes. He had a whole day of school ahead of him, and all he could think about was his bed.

Francisco felt better by break time, but he still couldn't keep up with his friends, who were rollerskating. Instead, he watched Dona play with a yo-yo. "Aren't you a little old for toys?" Francisco teased.

"You're just jealous that you don't have a yo-yo," Dona teased back. "Hey, why are you so grouchy today?"

Francisco takes a break from rollerskating. He hasn't had much energy since his cousins arrived in Manila.

Francisco's cousins, José and Manuel, work at a sugar refinery in Manila.

"My cousins are in town, working at the sugar refinery," Francisco grumbled. "Our apartment is so crowded that I have to sleep on the floor. My cousins wake me up when they come in late from the movies."

"Well, they're family and your guests," Dona replied. "You have to make them feel welcome. Besides, they don't get to see movies in the countryside like we do here in Manila. I'm sure they'll repay your kindness. That's what *utang na loob* is all about."

Afternoon lessons flew by, and soon Francisco was walking home from school. He passed the market, where he saw several boys selling fruit and flowers. Francisco was grateful that his older brothers worked, so he could go to high school one day. Many of his friends, like the boys in the market, had to find jobs instead of finishing their studies.

As Francisco walked down the hallway toward his apartment, he heard loud voices. Surprised, he opened the door to find José and Manuel, his cousins, dancing with his grandparents and younger sister.

"Francisco!" they cried. "Join the party!"

"Party?" Francisco asked.

"Our going away party!" José said. "The work season finished today, and tomorrow we return to our village."

Manuel slipped something into Francisco's hand. "This is to say thank you to our dear cousin Francisco, who gave up his bed for us."

Francisco opened his hand and found a bright yellow yo-yo. All he could think to say was *"Salamat!"* or "Thank you!"

That evening, Francisco's family held a special farewell feast for their guests. His mother served everyone's favorite, chicken *adobo* with sweet potatoes and rice. Later, his grandparents told folktales, including one about a bird that created the world. That night, Francisco lay on his floor mat clutching his new yo-yo. He was happy that Dona was right about his cousins showing their gratitude. He was even happier that tomorrow he would be sleeping in his bed!

Like many Filipino families in big cities, Francisco lives with his mother, father, sister, and grandparents in a high-rise apartment building.

Glossary

ancestor A person from whom one is descended

archipelago A large group of islands

architecture The science and art of designing and constructing buildings

bamboo A long, woody grass with hollow stems

capital A city where the government of a state or country is located

colony An area controlled by a distant country

corruption Dishonesty, often in politics or business

current The flow of water along a certain path in the sea or ocean

custom Something that a group of people has done for so long that it becomes an important part of their way of life

denomination A religious group within a faith

export The selling of goods to another country

guerrilla A member of an independent military group that uses sabotage and terrorism to fight against invaders from other countries or their own government

immigrant A person who settles in another country

intermarried Having married someone of a different religion or ethnic group

kerosene A thin, light-colored oil that is made from petroleum

livestock Farm animals

martial art A sport that uses warlike techniques for the purposes of self-defense and exercise

missionary A person who travels to a foreign country to spread a particular religion

mosque A Muslim place of worship

port A place where ships load and unload cargo

prophet A person who is believed to speak on behalf of God

rebel A person who opposes a government or ruler

sheer Thin and fine enough to see through

suckling Still drinking its mother's milk, referring to an animal

trade A type of work done by hand that requires special skill

vendor A person who sells goods

World War II A war fought by countries around the world from 1939 to 1945

 # Index

1 2 3 4 5 6 7 8 9 0   Printed in the USA   0 9 8 7 6 5 4 3 2